Table of Contents

Animals Nearby

Animals Far and Wide

Seasons and Holidays

MOVE OVER, MOTHER GOOSE!

Finger Plays, Action Verses & Funny Rhymes

By Ruth I. Dowell
Illustrations by Concetta C. Scott

Gryphon House, Inc.
Mt. Rainier, Maryland

The author is available to conduct
workshops for schools and conferences.
For information please contact:

Pollyanna Productions
4700 Poplar St.
Terre Haute, IN 47803
(812) 877-3286

© 1987 by Ruth I. Dowell

Published by Gryphon House, Inc., 3706 Otis Street, Mt. Rainier,
Maryland 20712.
Library of Congress Catalogue Card Number 87-82434

Design: Graves, Fowler & Associates

People & Places

Cooking and Eating

Home and Family

Fun and Games

Color & Numbers

Introduction

Children love rhythm. They express that love of rhythm naturally with movement. The rhymes in this book provide teachers with the opportunity to add rhythm and movement to classroom groups through the use of fingerplays and structured action verses. These activities help children to develop creativity and to experience greater self-esteem; and they promote and encourage verbal and motor skills. With this material, language becomes a pleasurable experience. Fingerplays such as "Where is Thumbkin?" bring small motor skills into play, whereas action verses such as "Ring Around the Roses" call upon larger muscles. With large body motions more suitable for younger children, and hand and finger motions more easily accomplished by older children, choices can be made to suit particular class needs.

Any rhyme in this book can be used either as a fingerplay or as an action verse. Fingerplays are best used when there is limited space for movement, i.e., with children seated or when a quieting activity is in order. Use fingerplays, for example, before or after lunch.

Action verses, since they involve whole-body movement, require more space and are most effective with children standing. The children may be in a circle, a line or wherever there is sufficient room to move. Such an activity is a relaxing transition between times of the day or a welcome change after a long quiet period.

Motions that accompany the rhymes should be creative and expressive, yet simple. Whether corresponding to individual words or to the meaning of the rhyme, one or two motions for each line of the rhyme is sufficient. Joining hands and walking in a circle, clapping hands or snapping fingers can be used for non-specific movement. The teacher should memorize each rhyme and its movement before presenting it to the class. With motor involvement providing the neurological imprint that speeds learning and repetition of rhythm and rhyme delivering pleasurable verbal stimulation, children easily remember these "story friends." The fingerplays and action verses should be recited rhythmically, as it is rhythm that will endear them to children as they respond to the whimsical nature of the characters featured in this book.

Once learned, these fingerplays and action verses contribute not only to group cohesion, but also provide children with creative suggestions to bring to their individual free play. In addition, the children may add their own creative interpretations to the verses. For example, in the rhyme about a cat named "Mr. O'Malley," a child may like to use the name of his own cat. The teacher can then repeat the verse, substituting the name of the child's pet. Another child may suggest a different hand or body motion. The teacher can personalize rhymes by substituting and inserting the name of a child in the class. (However, a word of caution: substitutions of this nature will need careful handling to maintain continuity and order, and, if attempted, should not be considered until each member of the class has mastered the original version.) Children should be encouraged to use a natural tone of voice, with variations that can include softer tones and a slower or faster rate.

While fingerplays and action verses are most often used at structured times, such as "circle time," they can be invaluable during waiting periods: to go outside, before snacks, before dismissal, etc. A rhyme can be a signal for a particular classroom activity. It's also a way for individual children through solo performances to demonstrate verbal skills and pride in accomplishment to classmates and family members.

The pleasure and usefulness of these wonderful, whimsical rhymes is yours to experience and is limited only by the imaginations of teacher and child.

Animals
Nearby

A Friendly Frog

ACTION VERSE
Children stand in a circle

*Move in a circle leaping around and
around like frogs*

A friendly frog lives in our pond
And croaks the night away:

Continue leaping

"Nee-deep, nee-deep; I never sleep,"

Continue leaping

Is what he seems to say.

Squat down and sit like frogs

He sits upon his lily pad
With darkness all around,

Rest head on both hands held together

And just before I fall asleep,

Cup hand to ear

I hear his friendly sound:

Get up and leap around again

"Nee-deep, nee-deep, nee-deep."

Junior the Frog

ACTION VERSE
Children stand in a circle

Jump into center of the circle

Junior the Frog jumped into the pond.

Place hands over head

The water was over his head!

Put finger on chin & cock head to one side

Now give him a minute; he'll surely
   remember:

Cock head to one side

What was it the mother frog said??

Jump into circle again

"You jump in a pond; the water is deep,

Shake head "no"

But that isn't bad—it's not bad!

Kick right leg and wiggle foot then repeat motion with the left leg and foot

Just kick with your legs and wiggle your feet!

Jump backwards twice

That's how you get back to the pad!"

A Poodle in a Fuddle

ACTION VERSE
Children stand in a circle

Look from left to right

A poodle in a fuddle
In the middle of a puddle!

Step left

Will he wade to the left?

Step right

Will he wade to the right?

Step into the middle

Will he stay in the middle

Point up to the sun

Till the sun shines bright?

Hold hands over head to form sun

When the sun shines bright,

Crisscross arms and move one left, one right

Will the puddle disappear?

Point to floor in front where standing

Will the poodle in the middle

Cup hands to mouth and say this louder, as though cheering

Give a great, big cheer?!

A Frog on a Log

FINGERPLAY
*Children are sitting. The right hand held in a loose fist is the frog
and the left arm extended out in front is the log.*

Place right fist on left arm   A frog on a log in a cranberry bog;

"Frog" hops up & down & looks around   A lonely old frog in a bog on a log.

"Frog" leans over "log"   He won't eat the berries; he will get a drink.

"Frog" hops up and down more   He'll be there till midnight or morning,
       I think.

In a Puddle

FINGERPLAY
Children are sitting

Raise up a little and sit back down   In a puddle sat a duck,

Put hands in armpits and flap arms   Flapped her wings and said, "Cluck, cluck!"

Wag finger from side to side   "That's not a duck," said Uncle Ben;

Make pecking motion with head   "No duck says 'cluck'; that chick's a HEN!"

Uncle Fumble Bumble Bee

Children form a circle and "fly around"

Uncle Fumble Bumble Bee began to buzz around.

With outstretched hands and arms make two circular motions, and then stoop down

He circled once, he circled twice, and landed on the ground.

Take a step in a stooped position

He took a step and saw he wasn't getting anywhere;

Stand up; fly around again, then stop and point

So, up he flew! (well, wouldn't you?)
And now he's over there!

A Handsome Deer

Stand with legs spread out slightly

A handsome deer
Was standing here
With antlers pointed high.

Place hands (with fingers outstretched) on top of head

Turn and face out of circle

He turned and ran!

Place hand (palm down) on chest

Why does he fear

Keep hand on chest

Someone as tame as I??

12

Bunnies

ACTION VERSE
Children are standing

Thump foot, jump in place

Twitch nose

Place hands on head for ears

Make "ears" go flip-flop

Bunnies like to thump and jump and
Twitch their noses when they stop.
Tails are short, but ears are long, and
Sometimes they will go flip-flop!

Robert the Rabbit

FINGERPLAY
Children are sitting

*Put head forward with hands on head
for ears*

Look to right and left

*Hold hands close together for "skinny",
then arms form a circle for "fat"*

Bite and crunch "carrot"

Robert the Rabbit peeked out of his pen,

Wondering, wondering, wondering, when
Someone or somebody, skinny or fat,

Would bring him a carrot, or something
   like that!

In a Barn

FINGERPLAY
Children are sitting

Place hands together to form roof	In a barn
Cup left hand to form nest	On a nest
Form right hand to be hen and sit it on left-hand nest	Sat a hen
	On-the-job
	With an egg
Lift up right hand and then count eggs	(Make it TWO!)
Surprise!—open mouth and put hand over it	And an old doorknob.
Shake head "no"	Well, the knob didn't hatch,
Lift up right hand "hen" from left hand nest again	But the two eggs hid
Take away right hand "hen" and place behind back, hold out only left-hand nest	In the nest
Place left hand nest behind back, then bring both hands back out to form roof, as above	In the barn
Stretch out arms to show large space for farm	on the farm
Nod "yes" firmly	SURE DID!

14

Alice the Cow

FINGERPLAY
Children are sitting

Moo, moo	"Well, now," said Alice the Cow.
Grab "hay"	Helping herself to some hay from the mow;
Put "hay" into mouth	"I'll just have a little-a little to munch,
Munch and munch	In case Farmer Brown should forget to serve lunch."

This Old Cow

ACTION VERSE
*Children stand in a circle. One child is in the middle as the cow. Another is chosen to be the new cow-man.
A third child is the "new cow," who becomes the old cow the next time around.*

Cow sits down	This old cow will give no milk!
Cow rests head on hands	We'll put her in a pen;
New cow-man comes into circle with a "new cow" and leads the "old cow" away. New cow becomes old cow.	And when the new cow-man comes 'round, We'll have to trade her in.

In a Stable

ACTION VERSE

Children stand in a circle. One child stands in the middle as the "donkey". The children in the outside circle join hands and walk around in a circle during the verse.

"Donkey" points to table and chair (real or imaginary)

In a stable stood a donkey
With a table and a chair.
Wonder why a donkey stable
Has a chair and table there??

"Donkey" chooses "company" from the outer circle to sit in the chair, and that person can become the next donkey.

Said the donkey, "Well, you know
The chair and table's not for me;
But a donkey never knows when he'll
Have 'people' company!"

In a Barnyard

ACTION VERSE
Children are standing

Put hands on head with fingers extended for the "horns" of the goat

In a barnyard stood a goat
Near the town of Terre Haute.

Rub chin   Caught his whiskers on a rail,
Rub behind   And got a splinter in his tail!

16

Come, Pet My Pony

ACTION VERSE
Children stand in a circle

Move around in a circle while galloping like horses

Come, pet my pony.
Pepita's her name.
You'll love her soft nose,

Shake head

And her long, shaggy mane.

Stop moving and stretch hand out tentatively (palm up)

She'll nibble the palm
Of your hand in a minute,
If only you hold

Stretch hand out all the way

Something sugary in it!

Gallop in a circle again

And, yes, you can ride her,

Hold "reins"

But DO hold on tight.
I don't think she'll buck,

Stop suddenly and jump

But you can't tell—she MIGHT!

Mr. O'Malley

FINGERPLAY
Children are sitting

Stroke "whiskers" on either side of mouth	Mr. O'Malley lives back in the alley,
Hold right arm out and then curl into self (like hugging) for the children & left arm for Mrs. O'Malley	Along with his children and Mrs. O'Malley.
Look proudly to right & left	Of sons and of daughters O'Malley has plenty.
Count to twenty	I counted them all and I found he has twenty!

Mrs. O'Malley

ACTION VERSE
Children stand in a circle

Walk lightly in a circle with backs hunched and arms hanging down	Mrs. O'Malley, You old alley cat! Why do you carry Your kittens like that?
Stop, pick up "kitten" from floor	I carry my kittens
Put "kitten" in mouth	The best way I know.
Walk around again	My babies go with me Wherever I go!

I'm Glad I'm Not

FINGERPLAY
Children sit. The mouse is the pinky on the right hand. The bat is both hands palm down & thumbs crossed. Flap hands up and down for the wings.

Make motion for mouse & then bat	I'm glad I'm not a mouse or bat!
Shake head "no"	I wouldn't want to look like that!
Make motion for mouse & then bat	But mice and bats, I'm sure agree
Point to self	They wouldn't want to look like "me!"

A Mouse Heard a Pussy Cat

FINGERPLAY
Children sit. The left hand is the cat. Hold this hand loosely closed with the first two fingers slightly extended. The pinky of the right hand is the mouse.

Move left hand slowly back and forth	A mouse heard a pussy cat moaning one day.
Cautiously, the pinky moves closer	The mouse, leaning closer, said, "What did you say?"
Move thumb and last 2 fingers of left hand	"I'm having a pain right here in my tooth. I feel rather awful, to tell you the truth.
Move fingers apart (to open "mouth")	I'll open my mouth" said the cat with a gleam; "And if you come closer, you'll see what I mean."
Pinky moves back and forth "no"	The mouse said, "I'm sorry your tooth hurts you so,
Pinky stops and stretches up straight and tall	But this is as close to a mouth as I go!"

Bennie the Beetle

FINGERPLAY

Children sit. The right hand is the beetle. It walks with the first two fingers.

	Bennie the Beetle!
Right fingers walk on left arm	O, he was so little
Jump up with hand	That crossing the sidewalk and back (Watch out!)
Walk slowly	Was always so tricky,
	In making the trip, he
Right hand falls off arm & then comes back up	Would often fall off in a crack! (Come back!)

ACTION VERSE

There are two lines of children. While saying the rhyme, they move toward each other. They reach each other on "Watch out", clap, and then move back to their orignal position. End with a clap on "Come back".

Caleb the Cricket

FINGERPLAY

Children sit. Left hand loosely closed with fingers spread apart is the thicket. Right index finger is the cricket.

Hold right index finger tightly in left hand and try to pull it out	Caleb the Cricket Was caught in a thicket.
Stop and sigh	He said, "I'm afraid it's no use;"
Poke finger through each of the four openings between fingers of closed hand	But all through the night, With all of his might,
Pull index finger out	He wiggled until he got loose!

Larry Had a Pet Canary

FINGERPLAY
Children are sitting

Hold both hands, palm down, thumbs locked, & flap hands up & down Larry had a pet canary,

Quickly move hands behind back Katy's kitty ate it!

Shake finger (Slowly) If you get a pet canary . . .

  (Quickly) Find a cage and cage it!

Move both arms quickly in front, clasp them together, as if catching the bird.

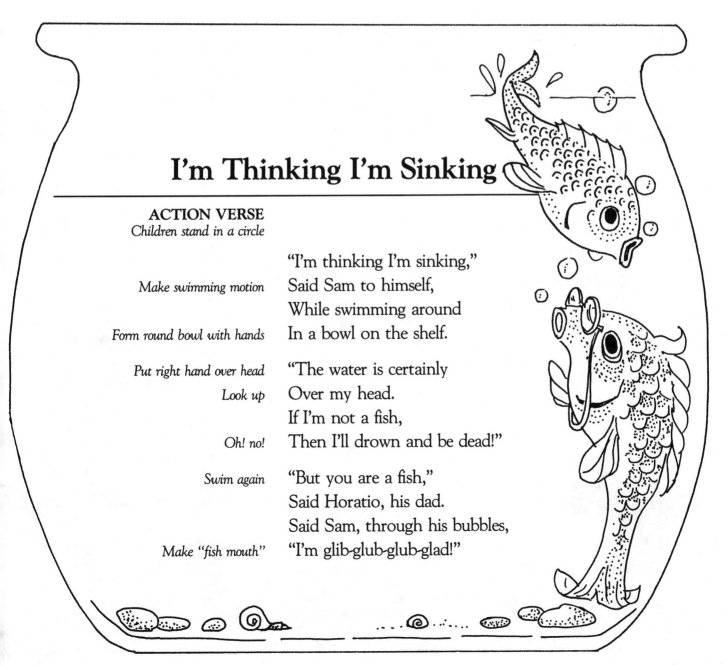

I'm Thinking I'm Sinking

ACTION VERSE
Children stand in a circle

  "I'm thinking I'm sinking,"

Make swimming motion Said Sam to himself,

  While swimming around

Form round bowl with hands In a bowl on the shelf.

Put right hand over head "The water is certainly

Look up Over my head.

  If I'm not a fish,

Oh! no! Then I'll drown and be dead!"

Swim again "But you are a fish,"

  Said Horatio, his dad.

  Said Sam, through his bubbles,

Make "fish mouth" "I'm glib-glub-glub-glad!"

Tabitha Cat

FINGERPLAY
Children are sitting

Stroke "whiskers" on face	Tabitha Cat
Ring "bell"	Has a bell on her hat—
Pat head	The one she wears in the house.
Put hand near ear	"O listen! How nice!
Hands on hips	How nice for the mice!"
Put hands (closed in fists) on top of head for mice ears	Said Ethyl, the old mother mouse.

Someone Call the Cat

ACTION VERSE
Children stand in circle

Cup hand near mouth to call cat	Someone call the cat!
Extend both arms out & shrug shoulders	The cat won't come—
Pour out "dinner"	Putthisdinnerinadishand
Push "dish" into circle	Give him some!
Put hand over eyes & look far away	Here comes the cat!
Move in circle taking tiny cat-like steps	Kitty pitter pat!
	Didyouknowthatyoucouldcatcha
	Cat like that??

22

Mortimer Rabbit

ACTION VERSE
Children are standing

Hop like a rabbit in place	Mortimer Rabbit Got into the habit
Stop, hold up two fingers and munch	Of eating two carrots a day.
Hold "carrot" in front of self	If you get a carrot,
Pass "carrot" to neighbor on right	You may want to share it
Hop, hop in place	With Mortimer. Whatta ya say? "Okay!"

A Mouse Chased a Pussy Cat

FINGERPLAY
The right hand is the cat & the left-hand pinky is the mouse.

	A mouse chased a pussy cat
Right hand crawls up to the shoulder	Up on a chair.
Crawls to the top of the head	How very embarrassing! Look at him there:
Move right hand up and down slowly	A flabby, old tabby Right here in our house! I just can't believe it:
Move left pinky up & down proudly	Afraid of a mouse!

23

"What's That"

FINGERPLAY
Children are sitting

Hand to ear	The cat's
	Back!
	He's been
	Gone
	All night
Wag finger	Long!
	Where's he
Extend arms out and shrug	Been?
	Ask him,
	When
	He stops to
	Lick
Stroke "whiskers" on side of mouth	His whiskers:
	Quick!
Point down to bowl	His bowl is
	Empty!
	"Tell us
	Simply:
	Were you
Point to the right	Here?
	Were you
Point to the left	There?
	Tell us! You must tell us
Wag finger back and forth	Where!"
	Said the
	Cat,
Arms extended cross them in front & *then move them back to each other*	"Enough of
	That!
	You know, quite
	Well,
	I cannot
Arms extended in front with palms up	Tell!"
	Then, up he jumped on Gran'ma's lap,
Rest head on hands	To have himself a nice, long nap.

Said Father Mouse

FINGERPLAY

Children sit. Right hand closed loosely is Father Mouse & the three first fingers on the left hand are the mice.

Move right hand up and down	Said Father Mouse to three young mice:
	"Now listen here to my advice.
Move right hand behind self	Behind the flour sack on the shelf
	(I saw it there today myself!)
Right hand shakes in fright	Is something frightful—something bad—
	That smells of things you've never had,
Move fingers on left hand	Like peanut butter, bacon, cheese:
	It could be any one of these.
	So, do beware of smells so fine,
Move right hand up and down firmly	And don't go near that place to dine!
	Or, without warning, there could be
Make left hand disappear behind back	No little mice, instead of three!"

25

Timorous Tammy

FINGERPLAY
Children sit. Left hand closed like a claw with fingers apart is the cage. Right pinky is the mouse.

Timorous Tammy, the Tutwiler's mouse,

Right pinky moves inside left hand Is kept in a cage at the rear of the house.

Pinky "hides" When company comes, Tammy never
   gets out;

Pinky comes out & moves along left arm But otherwise, Tammy can scurry about.

Now, Timorous Tammy is easy to please:

"Eat" food while on arm She nibbles on lettuce; she nibbles
   on cheese.

"Drink" water while on arm She either has water or nothing to drink,

Snuggle pinky into neck And no other mouse is as happy, I think!

Mr. Kelly

FINGERPLAY
Children are sitting

Meow, meow	Mr. Kelly got a cat
Extend arms out from sides—"fat"	And the cat he got GOT FAT!
Blow up cheeks	Feed him hay
Chew	Twice a day
Shake head "no"	And he won't be fat—
	HE WON'T BE FAT—
Extend arms out at sides—"fat"	Like that!

Matt the Rat

ACTION VERSE
Children are standing

Hold hands under a fat belly	Matt the Rat was getting fat,
Wag finger	And so his mother said,
	"Tonight, instead of cheese, you get
Make a "yuck" face	Some oldy, moldy bread!"
Shake head "no"	Well, Matt the Rat did not like that
Stand up straight	'Cause he was fully-grown.
Hug self with arms	He made himself a nest of fur,
Run in place	And ran away from home!

Rover Met a Polecat

FINGERPLAY
Children sit. The right hand is Rover & the left hand is the polecat. Hold hands loosely together, with thumb and first two fingers touching.

Move the right hand a little and then the left	Rover met a polecat—
Bring right hand and left hand together	Met him nose to nose!
Move hands apart and then together	And if you have to meet one,
"Sniff" hands and then move each behind back	That's the best way, I suppose!

28

Sand Hill City

ACTION VERSE
Children stand in a circle.

Join hands and walk in a circle

Sand Hill City is a place I know,
Where the ants and the beetles and the big
bugs go!

Tiptoe quietly in a circle & then cup hand to ear

It's a mound, and it's round. It's a big
round mound.
You can get real close, and you won't hear
a sound!

Move into the circle and then back out, while holding hands

But they're there, all right, goin' in,
comin' out.

Clap! clap!

It's an in-and-out, bug-about town.
NO DOUBT!

In a Dapper Chapeau

ACTION VERSE
Children are in a circle. Two children are in the center of the circle. They are the cat and mouse. The rest of the children hold hands and move in a circle during the verse.

Mouse taps head

In a dapper chapeau

Mouse fixes "tie"

And a matching cravat,
A mouse went to dine

Cat licks lips and strokes "whiskers"

With a calico cat.

Mouse stands on tippy toes

The mouse was excited,

Mouse pats head

Clear up to his brim,
Until he found out that

Cat chases mouse in middle of circle

The meal was on him!

Misery, Misery

ACTION VERSE
Children are standing

Hand head down	"Misery, misery!" moaned the rat.
Rub stomach	"It's either go hungry or cope with the cat!
Look cautiously from side to side	Wherever I go there's danger because
Move hands like claws	The cat's out there lurking with long, open claws!"
Make boxing motion	I don't wanna fight him (I think he would win!),
Rub stomach	But, oh, I'm so hungry, I hate to give in.
Part hands slightly & peek through	I wonder if I could sneak out through a crack
Pick up "crumbs" & put into mouth	And pick up some crumbs for a much-needed snack??"
Aha!	"Create a diversion!" he said to himself.
Smile and lick lips	"And go for the goodies they keep on the shelf,"
Wonder, with finger on chin	(But how do you fool an old calico cat With nothing at all on his mind but a rat?!)
	"Forget it! On second thought, maybe if I
"Tighten belt" & suck in stomach	Just tighten my belt, I can barely get by.
	It's awful to live with a cat 'on your case:'
Hide with one hand over face, rub stomach with other hand & stomp feet in place.	You're hiding, you're hungry, you're stuck in one place!"

Uguly, Buguly

ACTION VERSE

There are two circles. The outer one is frogs. They hop up & down in place. The inner one has bugs, mosquitos, or gnats. They move quickly in a circle, holding hands.

Frogs move eyes around from side to side

Ug-u-ly, bug-u-ly, og-u-ly eyes!
Thurman the Frog looked around in
   surprise.

Frogs hop up and down

Only a moment ago he had seen. . .
Dozens of bugs and some gnats in between!

Frogs flick tongues

O what he'd give for a bug or a fly,
A gnat or mosquito, if one would fly by!

Frogs smile & chew

Wait just a minute! He's eating! He's glad!
Tell me, O tell me what you think
   he had!
(A bug, a mosquito, a gnat or a fly??)

31

Fleagle the Beagle

FINGERPLAY
Children sit

Cup hands to mouth, as though calling	Fleagle the Beagle!
Point to "wrist watch"	It's time for the tub!
Point to self and then to "Fleagle"	I know you don't like it,
Make scrub motion with hands	But you need a scrub!
Make scrubbing circles	I'll wash you with soap
Point to "tail" and to "head"	From your tail to your head,
Hold arms out, palms up	And when you're all clean,
Rest head on hands	You can sleep on my bed.

My Doggie Has Fleas

FINGERPLAY
Children are sitting

Woof! Woof!	My doggie has fleas
Scratch nose and knees	From his nose to his knees
Slap fleas with two hands	More fleas than he ever could catch!
Sprinkle and spray motions	We sprinkled and sprayed him
Shrug	But nothing would save him!
Smile and scratch neck and arm	So, now, we just call him "Old Scratch!"
	(How's that?!)

Menominee

FINGERPLAY

Children sit. The right index finger is the flea.

Hold right finger up	Menominee, a hungry flea,
Move finger from side to side	Was looking for a place to be:
Move finger back & forth	A hairy dog, a furry cat;
Hold finger up straight	A place where he could hang his hat
Move finger around arm and upper body	And wander to his heart's content,
	With no one knowing where he went—
Touch arm with tip of finger	And have a bite by day or night
Hide finger behind arm	And stay completely out of sight.
	So, if your pet jumps on your bed
Move head from side to side	And asks you, please, to rub his head,
	Don't be surprised if you should see
Pop finger out from behind arm	That hungry flea, Menominee!

A Birdie Had a Dirty Beak

FINGERPLAY
Children are sitting

Hold hands with thumbs locked together, palms down, flap hands up & down	A birdie had a dirty beak.
Move thumbs down a little	He washed it in a muddy creek.
Move thumbs down again	The dirty beak did not come clean.
Flap hands & fly away	He should have picked a cleaner stream!

Kitty the Katydid

ACTION VERSE
Children hold hands in a circle

Crouch down and move in a circle	Kitty the Katydid hid in the grass, she did!
Move slowly into center of the circle	I wonder, wonder when she will come out again.
Move out & back in	When she comes out again, if she comes out again,
Stay in the center and whisper the last line	Then I can tell you when Kitty the Katydid did!

Dolly Duck

FINGERPLAY
Children are sitting

Make quack motion with no sound	Dolly Duck has lost her quack
Quack again with no sound	And wonders how to get it back.
Sip "tea"	"Just sip a little lemon tea,
Quack, quack with sound	And back will come your quack: you'll see!"

Animals
Far and Wide

Amanda is a Panda Bear

FINGERPLAY
Children are sitting

Make a circle with the first finger & *thumb of each hand & place over eyes*	Amanda is a panda bear;
Look from left to right	I saw her at the zoo. She's black and white like day and night
Hug self	And double-y, cuddle-y, too!

Lily's a Lady

FINGERPLAY
Children are sitting

Stroke "whiskers"	Lily's a lady, a lioness lady.
Lick "paws"	She lives with her mate in a lair.
Hold up right index finger	She may be a lady; but maybe, just maybe
Shake head "no"	You'd better not call on her there!

Don't Shake Hands with Tigers

FINGERPLAY
Children are sitting

Wag right finger back and forth	Don't shake hands with tigers, 'cause
"Claw" like a tiger	Tigers' paws have tiger's claws!

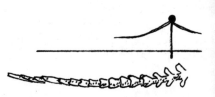

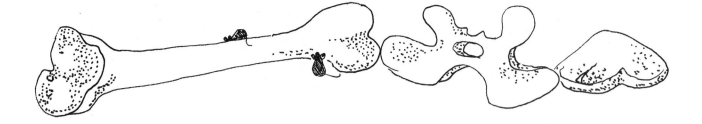

Once a Mighty Dinosaur

ACTION VERSE
Children are standing

Stand with head high	Once a mighty dinosaur
Sit down wearily	Sat down upon the jungle floor.
Put head on chest	He died, he did, without a name,
Boo hoo!	And no one cried. (Oh, what a shame!)
Move hands together from left to right	Then, many, many years went by.
Point to self from head to toe	The bones he left lay old and dry.
Dig, dig	They dug, they did, some time ago,
Point to self	And found his bones: that's how I know.
Show roof of big building	Now, somewhere in a big museum,
Stretch out arms	If you go there, you can see 'em:
Point left and right	Hundreds! Thousands! Maybe more!
Stand tall with head high	Enough to make a dinosaur!

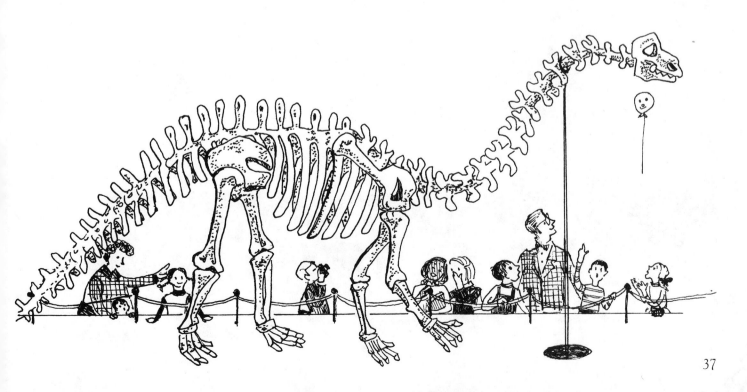

Billy Beaver

FINGERPLAY

Children are sitting

Swim with arms	Billy Beaver loved the water!
Shake hands with neighbor on right	Had a friend named Bobby Otter.
Put right hand over left, left over right, etc.	Built a dam;
Swim with arms	Swam and swam.
Hands on hips	Whatalottawaterforabeaverandanotter!

Ricky Raccoon

FINGERPLAY

Children sit. Put index fingers and thumbs together in a circle and hold over eyes.

	Ricky Raccoon is a bandit, they say.
Grab "things" from in front of self	He'll pilfer your vittles and scurry away!
Put circle over eyes	So if you go camping, watch out for this guy:
Wink	He'll snatch up your lunch in the wink of an eye!

A Lazy, Old Anteater

FINGERPLAY
Children are sitting

Put finger on chin	A lazy, old anteater couldn't decide
"Walk" right finger on left arm	Whether to walk to the anthill or ride.
Put finger on chin again	"Such decision; how nice it would be,
Curl finger toward self	If only the anthill would come here to me!"

A Muskrat

FINGERPLAY
Children are sitting

	A muskrat sat on an old tree stump,
Tip "hat"	And he tipped his hat to a passing skunk.
Surprise!, then wave "hi"	The skunk said, "Oh!", then he said, "Hello.
Point away	I would love to stay, but I have to go!
Look at "watch"	There's a Skunktown meeting, and I'm gonna be late;
	But I'll be right back if you care to wait."
	The muskrat said,
Sniff with nose	With a sniff (sniff, sniff!)
Scratch head	And a scra-tch-tch,
	"O, I just remembered:
Hold finger in air & wave bye, bye	I've a train to catch!"

Erma Pachyderm

ACTION VERSE
Children are standing

Walk heavily	Erma Pachyderm is a little overweight,
Each foot steps down hard	But the circus has her picture out in front.
Chew, chew	Everyday they feed her hay,
Puff cheeks out	So I guess she'll stay that way:
Put arms out to side to show fat	She's a roly-poly lady elephant!

Oliver the Elephant

ACTION VERSE
Children are standing

Sneeze	Oliver Elephant happened to sneeze,
Fall to knees	And all of a sudden he fell to his knees!
Struggle	It's hard to get up
Struggle and wipe brow	When you're built like a truck
Get up with ease	But Oliver did it with ease.

Penelope Elephant

FINGERPLAY
Children are standing

Look up

Sit down

Settle into sitting position

Drink "tea"

Look up & follow "umbrella" coming down slowly

Penelope Elephant's yellow umbrella
Got stuck in the top of a tree.
This elegant elephant lady decided
To have a cup of tea:
"I'll sip my drink and sit a while,
And soon the wind will blow;
And down will come my yellow umbrella
And off again I'll go."

Humpback

Make a big "hump" in front of self	Humpback! Whatta whale!
Big clap!	Splashed the water with his tail!
Cup hands to mouth	"Here I go!", I heard him say.
"Dive" with arms	Down he went and swam away!

Mickey the Mackerel

FINGERPLAY
Children are sitting

Move hands like waves	Mickey the Mackerel lives in the sea.
Put finger on chin, wondering	If someone catches him, where will he be??
Oh! no! two hands on cheeks	Cooked!. . .in a frying pan, wouldn't you say?
"Swim" away	"Quick, Mickey Mackerel! Swim away!"

Charlie Made a Doughball

ACTION VERSE

Children are standing in a circle. One child is in the middle of the circle. This is the shark.
The other children are "Charlies." They cast fishing poles.

Children in outer circle mold "doughballs"	Charlie made a doughball;
Put "doughballs" on hooks	Stuck it on a hook;
Cast pole into the circle	Threw it in the ocean,
Shark circles around and watches everyone	And a shark took a look.
Shark cups hand to mouth	"Hey, there, up there; Don't you know? I can't eat this
Shark makes "yuck" face	Mess o' dough!
Outer circle children cast poles	Throw me down a catfish! Any fish'll do! I could even make a meal of
Shark points to one child (This child can then become the shark.)	Y - O - U !"

Myrtle Was a Turtle

FINGERPLAY

Right hand is the turtle. Thumb and index fingers are the left feet. Pinky and ring fingers are the right feet & middle finger is the head.

Myrtle was a turtle

Right hand crawls on left arm   with a polka-dotted shell.

Move head up and move from side to side   She looked a little funny, but she managed very well.

Tap middle finger down twice   She ate a lotta bugs and a juicy worm or two,

Move right hand along arm   And she even went to live at the Children's Zoo.

ACTION VERSE

In a line or circle the children move slowly like turtles for the first stanza. They have smiles on their faces. For the second stanza they dip their heads down twice, each time coming up chewing. End with crawling.

A Penguin

ACTION VERSE
Children are standing

Waddle from side to side
Waddle first, then "swim"
Hold up two fingers
Tuck hands into armpits & "flap" wing

A penguin, when he goes somewhere,
Will walk or swim; here's why:
Although he has two bird-like wings,
He simply cannot fly!

Marco the Polar Bear

ACTION VERSE
Children are standing

Stand up in a circle
Extend out arms proudly
Sit down
Shiver

Marco the Polar Bear,
White as the snow,
Sat down on the ice
Near the cold water's flow.

Rub stomach
Put hands together to make a wish
Put right hand down
Hold up right hand and smile

"Lunch! I need lunch!" he said;
"I'll make a wish."
He stuck in his paw
And came up with a fish!

Tim O'Dare

FINGERPLAY
Children are sitting

Tim O'Dare

"Shoot" gesture   Shot a bear standing in his underwear.

Point left   Was it Tim,

Point right and gesture from neck to ankles   Or was the BEAR wearing underwear out there??

Odie Coyote

FINGERPLAY
Children are sitting

Odie Coyote, with ev-e-ry note, he

Form mouth into circle   Grew louder and LOUDER, until

Look fearfully from side to side   The moon disappeared and he suddenly feared

Hand over eyes, look off   That the sun would rise over the hill.

Make "sun" over head   Then up came the sun! See the coyote run,

Slap knees with right and left hands; continue   As he hides from the light of day!

Point up to "moon"   But later tonight, when the moon's shining bright,

Form mouth into circle   He'll be prowling and howling away!

One Fine Day

FINGERPLAY
Children are sitting

Put hand over eyes & look around   One fine day in the woods I saw...

Lick near palm of hand   A bear in a honey tree, lickin' his paw.

Move right pinky (bee) around in the air   A bee buzzed by, and what do you suppose?

Land pinky on nose   The bee stung the bear on the tip of his nose!

Rub nose with hand   "Ouch!" said the bear, as he slid down the tree;

Shake head "no"   "I DO like the honey, but I DON'T like the bee!"

Pierre the Bear

FINGERPLAY
Children are sitting

Hold hands together pleading   Pierre the Bear! O tell me where

Lick fingers   To look for honey trees.

If you don't mind, I'd like to find

Right pinky (bee) moves around and makes buzzing noise   The ones without the bees!

Matilda Gorilla

Bend over slightly and hang arms down	Matilda Gorilla lives deep in the jungle
Swing arms	Where she has a favorite place:
Sit down comfortably	She sits by a stream, very cool and serene,
Smile with chin in hands	And admires her gorilla-ry face.

In the Middle . . . Orange Orangutang

Crouch down and stretch arms up	In the middle of the jungle
Move around	where the tall trees grow,
Swing right arm out and back	There's a hairy, orange orangutang—
Repeat with left arm	you oughta see him go!
Move around	Well, his hairy arms are longer than
	the OTHER part of him;
Swing arms out in front & back	And he swings like a monkey
Swing arms as if using a jungle gym	in his jungle jungle gym.

48

Everyone Knows a Buffalo Grows

ACTION VERSE
Children are standing

Bend over from the waist down

Swing arms back and forth slightly

Pull up "zipper" & shake head "no"

Bring arms into body & hold tight

Everyone knows a buffalo grows
A shaggy, fur coat when the winter
   wind blows.
No buttons, no zippers; no, not anything!
But buffalo coats will stay fastened
   'til Spring!

Raleigh the Wallaby

ACTION VERSE

Two children hold hands over their heads to form a tent. The other children hop in a line and go through the "tent."

Raleigh the Wallaby rented a tent:
Oh, Raleigh the wallaby gent.
And when it got dark
He went to the park
And into his rented tent went!

If You Should Meet...Kangaroo

ACTION VERSE
Children are standing

Hang arms down in front like a kangaroo

Hop in place

Box chin

Box, box into middle of circle

If you should meet outside a zoo,
A kangaroo may corner you.
He'll box your chin and maybe win
If you don't get the best of him!

A Crocodile

ACTION VERSE

Stand in line with hands on the shoulders of person in front.

Take tiny, tiny steps	A crocodile could walk a mile,
Continue as above	But it would take him quite awhile.

An Alligator

ACTION VERSE

Children hold hands in a circle

Squat down and slowly stand up	An alligator went to take an elevator ride.
Take one step into circle	Said the elevator operator, "Step inside."
Up on toes then down on heels	First floor, second floor, up and down:
Squat down and slowly stand up	It's the only alligator elevator in town!

A Boa Constrictor

FINGERPLAY

Children sit. Right hand is the boa constrictor; left hand is the sister. Each hand is held loosely closed with fingertips and thumb meeting together to form a snake head.

Move right hand	A boa constrictor
Move left hand	May look like his sister,
Shake both hands "no"	But don't make a fatal mistake:
Move right hand	A boa constrictor
Move left hand	Can look like his sister
Shake both hands "yes"	And still be a dangerous snake!

Duckbill Platypus

ACTION VERSE
Children are standing

Hands on stomach, ha!, ha!	"Duckbill Platypus!" Lotta fun to say!
Jump to one side	But if you should run into one, get out of his way!

51

Ringo Flamingo

ACTION VERSE
Children are standing

Stand tall and proud

Pick up right leg & hold it up, then put down

Repeat with left leg

Tuck hands in armpits & "flap wings"

Ringo Flamingo, a bird with a flare,
Stands tall in the water and
wades everywhere.
His color is pink, with a slight touch
of black.
He may fly away, but I think he'll
come back.

Alexander Salamander

FINGERPLAY
Children sit. Right index finger is the salamander & left arm is the limb.

Rest right finger on left arm

Move right finger rhythmically, as in sleep

Move right finger faster (breathing gets harder)

Alexander Salamander,
Sleeping on a limb,
Dreamed there was an alligator
Coming after him!

Lift up finger horizontally

Move from side to side

Move second finger onto arm

When he got awake, he found
No alligator there:
Just another salamander
Coming up for air.

Seasons
And Holidays

Mr. Pumpkin (Hello)

FINGERPLAY
Children are sitting

Wave "hello"	Mr. Pumpkin! Well, hello!
	You're back again this year!
Point to eyes, then to nose	I see your eyes; I see your nose;
Trace grin on face with finger	You're grinning ear to ear!
Curve left arm around	Inside we'll put a candle stick
Put right hand into curve of left arm	To make a lantern light;
Move left (curved) arm onto floor or lap	Then, set you on the old front porch
Hold both arms out, palm up	And let you shine all night!

Mr. Pumpkin (Goodbye)

FINGERPLAY
Children are sitting

Wave bye, bye	Mr. Pumpkin, well, goodbye.
Make "come back" motion	Come back again next year.
Hand over eyes & look off in distance	There's someone coming down the road.
Roll hands over each other	He's getting very near.
Look around to your back	With feathers all around his tail,
Cup hand near ear	I think I hear him say,
	"When I get there, then everywhere
Extend both arms out, with palms up	We'll have THANKSGIVING DAY!"

Itchy McGitchy

ACTION VERSE
Children are standing

Move stealthily in a circle	If Itchy McGitchy the Goblin should getcha,
Tickle self under chin	Just tickle him under his chuck-a-luck chin.
Laugh	He'll laugh and he'll dropya, as tho' he forgotcha,
Rest head on hands	And you'll be back in your bedroom again!

With Icicles Hanging

FINGERPLAY
Children are sitting

Dangle fingers down like icicles	With icicles hanging in nice, little rows,
Cover nose with hand	You'd best button buttons and cover your nose!
Pat head	DO wear your mittens and hat, if you please,
Ah choo!	And hurry inside if you happen to sneeze!

Old Man Weatherby

ACTION VERSE
Children are standing

Step twice in place	Old Man Weatherby walks or not,
Wipe brow	Depending on whether the weather is hot.
Shake head "no"	Cold or snow-he won't go:
Hold arms around self and shiver	He doesn't have an overcoat, don't you know!

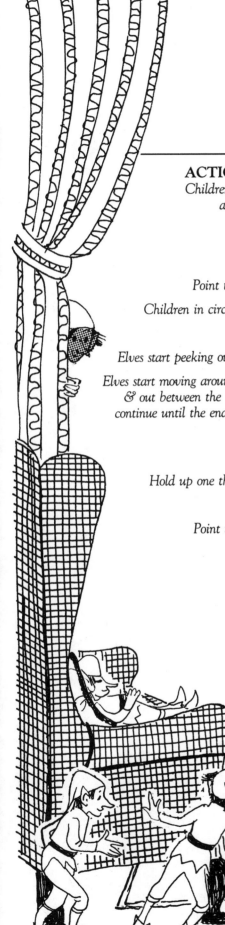

Santa Claus

ACTION VERSE

Children stand in circle, leaving space between each other. Four children are elves. They start out behind the circle, scattered around.

	Santa Claus is coming!
Smile	I can feel it in the air!
Point to someone else	And, maybe you don't know it,
Children in circle look around	But his elves are everywhere:
	Hiding in the corners,
Elves start peeking out from behind	Peeking out with twinkly eyes!
Elves start moving around, weaving in & out between the children. They continue until the end of the rhyme.	Will they see you being nice, Or being OTHERwise?
	I would like a present—
Hold up one then two fingers	Maybe even TWO!
	Anyone can see I'm being good;
Point to someone else	Are you??

57

Pitter, Patter, Scatter

FINGERPLAY
Children are sitting

Pitter, patter, scatter!

Wiggle finger in front like "rain"   See the raindrops on the wall,

Crowding one another, till

Move fingers faster   There's room enough for all!

Move arms in small circles at sides   Water, water raining,

Making rivers in the street:

Continue making circles with arms, while bringing them to front & overlap circles   Flooding, rushing water

Where the avenues meet!

ACTION VERSE
For the first stanza, tiptoe slowly around in a circle, making it "rain" in front of you with your fingers. For the second stanza, keep increasing the pace of movement until the end when it suddenly stops.

I Hear Thunder

FINGERPLAY
Children are sitting

Clap on "thunder", then put hands on ears   I hear thunder! It's no wonder

Make "rain" come down   All that rain keeps coming down!

Put finger on chin, wondering   Is the weather any better

Point to "other side"   On the other side of town?

Fletcher the Weatherman

FINGERPLAY
Children are sitting

Hold hand out palm up   Fletcher the Weatherman says it will rain,

Look up to sky   And there is a cloud in the sky. (He's right!)

Hold "umbrella" in right hand   I'll take my umbrella, my yellow umbrella,

Extend arms out, palms up   And go out and come back dry! "Goodbye!"

Climbing Up the Apple Tree

ACTION VERSE
Children are standing

"Climb" in place	Climbing up the apple tree,
Raise arms above head, sway left & right	Swinging on a limb!
Cup hand near ear	If I hear a robin, I may
Sing tra la la	Sing along with him!
Put hand over eyes	"And Robin, if you fly away,
Hold index finger	Here's what I think I'll do:
Gently flap arms at side & move around	I'll wish a pair of sparrow wings
	And fly away with you!"

I See Something (Easter Bunny)

ACTION VERSE
Children are standing

Hop in a circle	I see something fat and furry
Continue hopping	In a flurry, in a hurry!
Stop and make "sun" with arms	On this morning bright and sunny
Put finger on chin	Could it be the Easter Bunny?
Hop again	Yes, it is! O how he races,
Place right finger on lips	Hiding eggs in secret places!
Point	Do you see one? Yessiree!
Place right hand down and bring up "egg"	In the hollow of a tree!

'Way Last Summer

ACTION VERSE

One child is the scarecrow in the middle of the circle. The other children stand.

Raise hands up tall	'Way last summer, when the corn grew tall,
Scarecrow stands up tall	Stood an old scarecrow in the middle of it all.
Make "rain" with hands and blow for "wind"	Well, the sun and the wind and the rain came down,
Scarecrow puts hand over eyes & looks around	And the scarecrow watched as the corn turned brown.
Chop, chop	So, the farmer cut the corn, and the field was bare;
Scarecrow looks sad	And the old scarecrow was the only thing there.
Blow, blow hard	Then the winter wind blew and the field turned white.
Scarecrow turns and looks around	Still, the scarecrow stood, like a soldier, day and night.
Children bend down and touch ground	Then the springtime came and the farmer plowed the ground,
Scarecrow smiles	And the scarecrow smiled, but he didn't make a sound.
Raise hand a little off the floor	Now, the corn's still young, so it isn't very tall,
Scarecrow puts hands on hips & all children shake head "no"	And the scarecrow waits, but he doesn't mind at all!

60

Summer

ACTION VERSE
Children are standing

	In the summer
Run in place	I'm a runner.
Leap in place	I'm a leaper.
Jump in place	I'm a jumper.
Kick foot	I'm a player.
Sit down slightly	I'm a rider.
	I'm an always-stay-outsider!
Jump up and slap thighs with hands	I'm a romper.
Tap, tap ground	I'm a camper.
Throw ball	I'm a pitcher.
Catch ball	I'm a catcher.
"Swim"	I'm a swimmer.
"Dive" with arms	I'm a diver.
Jump into position with arms and legs stretched out	In the summer I'm alive!

VARIATION
Have eleven solo voices, one for each line, with ALL saying the last statement of each stanza.

61

I Went to Nantucket

FINGERPLAY
Children are sitting

	I went to Nantucket
Dig, dig	To fill up my bucket with sand,
Make "wave" with hands	But a wave came ashore!
Sigh	Now woe is me!
Hold hands out, palms up	My bucket's asea!
Wave bye,bye	No sand and no bucket no more!
	(Poor me!)

Oh! To be . . . Beach

FINGERPLAY
Children are sitting

Sigh	Oh! To be on a sandy beach
Make "waves" with arms	And watch the waves come in!
Raise two fingers	Then, take a step or two and feel
Tap under chin	A wave splash under my chin!
"Dig" with hands	And, on the shore to dig a hole
"Build" castle on lap	Or build a castle there!
Point to another person	So, if YOU'D like to come, come on!
Make "come on" motion	There's more, much more, to share!

People
And Places

Everybody Out the Door

ACTION VERSE
Children are standing

Make "come on" motion	Everybody out the door!
Take one step forward	All aboard for Singapore!
	Are we going in our car?
Move in circle	Let's get rolling if we are!
Move more slowly	Both front tires could use some air.
Stop	Don't forget to air the spare!
Pump up "tire"	There's a station; stop right here!
	Both front tires are flat, I fear.
Repeat "pumping"	Pump them up, and if they stay,
Wipe brow	We will soon be on our way.
Lean foot up on heel & then press down	Press the pedal; shift the gear!
Move in circle again	Look at this: We're here! We're here!

Steamroller, Roadgrader

Children are in a line. They hold onto the waist of the child in front of them. Everyone steps in unison, first right, then left, and so on. Take heavy steps.

Steamroller, roadgrader!
You can I know!
Build me a highway to
Anywhereiwannago!

A Rocket

FINGERPLAY
Children are sitting

Hold right hand with first two fingers pointed up on left palm

A rocket is what
An astronaut

Raise right hand up and away

Must have to get to the moon.

Bring arms together and then spread them out to each side

A spaceship is where
He lives while he's there.

Point to another person

Will you be going there soon?

In the Mountains

ACTION VERSE
Children are standing

Swing right hand onto shoulder and walk

In the mountains was a man
With a pick and a pan,

Shade eyes with left hand

And he looked for gold

Shiver

Where the stream ran cold.

Point nearby and then far away

Well, he picked over here—and he panned over there,

Hold out hands & shrug shoulders

But he didn't find gold—
NOT A NUGGET ANYWHERE!

Swing right hand onto shoulder & pick up "pack" with left hand

So he packed up his pick, and he picked up his pack,

Walk again and shake head "no"

And he went to the city,
AND HE NEVER CAME BACK!

66

Pennsylvania Pete

ACTION VERSE
Children stand in a circle

(Children can easily learn the responses in parenthesis.) Walk in a circle, snapping toes. Children stop at the end of each two lines and say the responses.

Pennsylvania Pete had a pair of handy feet,
And they took him any place he had to go.
  (How so?)
When the weather was nice or the streets
    were ice,
In the rain, in the sleet, or in the snow.
  (Let's go!)

Well, he didn't have the money, so he didn't
    have a car,
And he didn't have a horse and sleigh;
  (Okay!)
But it didn't really matter 'cause he didn't
    like the clatter,
And his feet didn't eat any hay!
  (No way!)

VARIATIONS
Children can clap for the responses.

Mr. Pocatella

ACTION VERSE
Children stand (Saying the words in parenthesis will add to the enjoyment)

Limp in a circle holding right arm stiff Mr. Pocatella had a leaky um-ber-ella
And he carried it and used it as a cane.
  (Good bet!)

Shake head "no" It was dandy as a crutch, but it didn't help
  him much

Hold hand out, palm up & frown When the fella had to stand out in the rain!
  (Got wet!)

Mistopher Christopher

FINGERPLAY
Children are sitting

Make "roof" with hands Mistopher Christopher lives on a hill,

Hold hand with index finger and thumb slightly apart And his house was too little, too little until

Reach behind back with each hand & bring to front He got him some boards and some other
  good stuff,

Make "big roof" with hands And hammered until it was just big enough!

Tolliver Tidewater

ACTION VERSE
Children are standing

Make "roof" with hands   Tolliver Tidewater lives in a shack,
Move hand in front & back   With a dirt road in front and a path
                 in the back.
Pet "dog"   He has an old dog with a stub of a tail;
Hold hands & move in circle   Together, they walk into town for the mail.
      And, if he has any, and, if it's a bill,
Shrug shoulder   If he doesn't pay it, then someone else will!
Skip in circle   He hasn't a worry; he hasn't a care:
      He lives for today; let tomorrow beware!

Hee-haw Havachaw

FINGERPLAY
Children are sitting

Cast "fishing pole" twice

Hee-haw Havachaw
Was a man from Arkansas.
Worked a little;
Played a little;

Grab "fish" from line and put in mouth

Caught a fish and ate it raw!

VARIATION
Exaggerate the vowels

I Think I'll Go to Tim-buc-tu

ACTION VERSE
Children are standing

Walk, walk, walk in place	I think I'll go to Tim-buc-tu,
	If there is such a place;
"Comb" hair	But, first, I'd better comb my hair,
Rub face	And, maybe, wash my face.
Take a step to the right	I wonder: should I take a bus
Take a step to the left	Or get aboard a train?
	But, if it's very far away,
Take a step forward	I'd better take a plane!
	I need to pack a suitcase.
Put finger on chin, wondering	Is the weather cold or hot??
Shiver	And will I need long underwear,
Fan self	Or summer clothes, or what?!
	There's such a lot to think about—
Scratch head, confused	So many things to do...
	I may decide, instead, that I
Shake head "no"	Won't go to Tim-buc-tu!

Mr. Fiddle Faddle

ACTION VERSE

Children stand in a circle. (Children will enjoy this rhyme even more when they say the responses in parenthesis.)

Gallop in a circle	Mr. Fiddle Faddle had a rattle in his saddle,
Pat side twice on "of course"	And he took it to the saddle-rattle man. (OF COURSE!)
Gallop in a circle	Said the saddle-rattle man, "I will fix it if I can;
Pat side twice on "say how"	Tell me how this saddle-rattle all began." (SAY HOW!)
Stop, sit with legs slightly apart	"Well, I got my saddle rattle when I sat astride the saddle
Put hand on open mouth for "o my"	And the cattle, when they heard the rattle, ran! (O MY!)
Rub chin	Said the saddle-rattle man, "That's a problem, Cattle Man;
"Steer" jeep, put hands on hips for "o yes"	And I think you ought to buy yourself a jeep!" (O YES!)
Put arms out with palms up	Well, he tried to buy a jeep, but the prices were too steep,
Put chin on fist for "o dear"	And he couldn't find a cheap jeep anywhere! (O DEAR!)
Strecth arms out & smile	Then a fella said he would Buy the cattle where they stood,
Clap, clap	So he sold the herd and moved to Delaware! (ALL RIGHT!!)

A Clown

ACTION VERSE
Children are standing

Stretch clothes out at hips
Snap down toes of right & left feet
Tap, tap nose

A clown you can tell
By the look of his clothes,
The shape of his shoes and
The size of his nose!

Firman the Fireman

ACTION VERSE
Children are standing

Cup hand to mouth & then make "come on" motion

Firman the Fireman! I need you!
  Come quick!

Fan smoke & cough

Something is burning! The smoke's
  getting thick!

Squirt "hose"

Do bring the hose; and, of course,
  wear your hat!

Raise up four fingers individually

And you'll have the fire out in four
  minutes flat!

Mr. Blinken

FINGERPLAY
Children are sitting

Put finger to forehead — Mr. Blinken, I been thinkin'
Make a small circle in the air near head — What a funny man you are!

Point to self and then to another — I have noticed that you always
Open mouth, put hand over mouth & giggle — Drive your hat and tip your car!

Mr. Tickle Lickle

FINGERPLAY
Children sit. Children can easily learn the responses: "Tweet, tweet!" and "Some hat!"

Hold "feather" in front — Mr. Tickle Lickle bought a feather for a nickle
Put "feather" on head — And he stuck it in the middle of his hat. (TWEET! TWEET!)
Fly arms like a bird — Now, he's singing like a bird—like a bird you never heard!
Pat head — And he only paid a nickle! Think of that! (SOME HAT!)

Mr. Taller Timber

ACTION VERSE
Children are standing

Swing "axe" onto shoulder	Mr. Taller Timber took his axe to the woods,
Chop, chop	And he chopped on a tree just as hard as he could!
Chop and wipe brow	But, the tree didn't fall, didn't move— not at all!
Shake head "no"	So he couldn't get the wood he should've.
Hold both arms out, palms up & shrug	That's all.

Listen!...Mr. Fat

ACTION VERSE
Children are standing

Cup hand near ear	Listen! Have you heard the news?!
Hold arms out at sides to show "fat"	Mr. Fat can't tie his shoes!
Hold index finger up	I know what he'll have to do:
"Slip" into "shoes"	Wear the kind you slip into!

75

Mr. Haber Dasher

FINGERPLAY
Children are sitting

Hold up pinky   Mr. Haber Dasher was a little bitty guy,

Almost cover pinky with other hand   But he had a heavy hat: about a
twenty-gallon size!

Move two hands around together   Well, I never saw him anywhere without his
heavy hat,

Rest head on hands   And I wonder if he went to bed a-lookin'
like that!

Finnerty Haggerty

FINGERPLAY
Children are sitting

Pat & stroke head   Finnerty Haggerty bought a fur hat.

Point to another person's head   Said Finnerty's wife, when she saw it,
"What's that?!"

Pat head   "I bought it," he told her, "to wear on
my head."

Open mouth & put hand over it   Said Finnerty's wife, "Is that animal dead??!"

I Haven't the Faintest...Ocean

FINGERPLAY
Children are sitting

Hold hands out, palms up & shrug shoulders
I haven't the faintest, the foggiest notion

Right hand pours "water"
How somebody managed to fill up the ocean

Stretch arms out to both sides
And all of the rivers and lakes that abound

Dig, dig
And all of the holes that are dug in
   the ground!

Frown, put finger on chin
And sometimes I worry a little (do you??)

Open mouth, put hands on both cheeks
That someone may suddenly empty
   them, too!

Bim! Bam! Alakazam!

FINGERPLAY
Children are sitting

Bim! Bam! Alakazam!

Roll hands over each other
A man in a barrel went over a dam!

Move index finger along "a line" as if reading
He did it for money, the newspapers said:

Point to pockets & then to head
His pockets were empty AND SO WAS
   HIS HEAD!

Donnie Diego

ACTION VERSE
Children are standing

Limp in a circle
Look down & point to floor
Walk with a limp again
Shake finger

Donnie Diego has broken his leg! Oh,
He went through a hole in the floor. "Poor
Donnie Diego, you've broken your leg! Oh,
You should have gone out through the door!"

Silly Billy

FINGERPLAY
Children are sitting

Hold bundle of "hay" in front
Drop hay & start "pitching" it
Extend hand out to feed "horse"
Move hand to mouth and chew

Silly Billy bought some hay
From a farmer yesterday.
With the hay, he fed his horse
And ate the rest himself, of course.

Mr. Pickett

ACTION VERSE
Children are standing

Hand "ticket" into circle	Mr. Pickett bought a ticket,
Turn to right and take one step	Got aboard a bus.
Skip around	He went to Disneyworld, I think,
Stop and rub both eyes (boo, hoo)	And went there without us!

Herbert the Hobo

ACTION VERSE

There are two circles. The outer one is the train. The inside smaller one is hobos. The train circle holds onto each other's shoulders & shuffles feet. Each time "hopped" is said, one hobo moves onto the train circle. Repeat until all hobos are on the train.

Herbert the Hobo, he hopped on a train
And he lived in a boxcar from Georgia
   to Maine!
They didn't collect and he didn't pay rent.
He followed the engine wherever it went!

Little Old Lady

FINGERPLAY
Children are sitting

Pat head	Little old lady, I like your new hat!
Point to someone's head	Where did you pick up a beauty like that?
Cup left hand & reach into it with right	"I bought it," she said, "at a neighborhood sale
Take out something twice	For twenty-five cents and a ten-penny nail!"

This Old Car

ACTION VERSE
Children are in a circle holding hands

Move slowly, stop and sit	This old car is out of gas!
Point to someone in the circle	Go and get some, Mrs. Bass.
Pour "gas"	Pour it in.
Get up	Go again.
Move again in circle	Move on over; let me pass!

Cooking
And Eating

Billy Mahoney

ACTION VERSE
Children are standing

Smile Billy Mahoney eats only baloney;
Bite and chew He has it for lunch every day!
Will Billy Mahoney turn into baloney,
If Billy keeps eating that way?

Open mouth and put hand over mouth Oh, oh, yes . . .

Blow cheeks out & hold arms out at sides Billy Mahoney turned into baloney!
I knew it would happen—it did!
Walk in place, waddling from side to side Now, Billy Mahoney is Billy Baloney:
A hunk-of-a, chunk-of-a-kid!

Tom Had a Turnover

FINGERPLAY
Children are sitting

Put hand to mouth	Tom had a turnover;
Chew	Kim preferred pie;
Bring hand to mouth	Jill ate some jelly and
Chew	Bread—so did I.
	Now, what would you like?
Shiver for cold & "ouch" for hot	Something cold? Something hot?
Put finger on chin, wondering	It's time to be choosey.
Point to "something"	Decide, and say what!

Eat an Apple

ACTION VERSE
Children are standing

Bring right hand to mouth	Eat an apple;
Close right hand in fist	Save the core.
Bend down touch hand to ground	Plant the seeds
Extend both arms out	And grow some more!

If I Only Had a Nickel

FINGERPLAY
Children are sitting

Sigh	If I only had a nickel
Smile	I would buy myself a pickle
Hold out left hand, palm up	And I'd put it in the middle
	Of a sandwich with a little
Put right hand on top of left	Bit of butter and baloney
Move both hands together to mouth	And I'd eat it, if I only
Sigh	Had a nickel
Smile	For a pickle—
Sigh	But I don't!

84

Aunt Matilda

FINGERPLAY
Children are sitting

Hold both hands out together, palms up	Aunt Matilda baked a cake.
"Stir cake"	(She baked a cake, you say?)
Repeat	Yes, Aunt Matilda baked a cake
Lick lips	A chocolate one, TODAY!
Move hand to mouth	So, Aunt Matilda ate the cake.
Chew	(She ate it by herself??)
Rub stomach, hmm good	No, Aunt Matilda ate SOME cake
Put "cake" on shelf	And put some on the shelf.
	Well, Aunt Matilda went away.
Lean forward & raise eyebrows	(She left her little house?)
	Yes, Aunt Matilda went away
Right pinky (mouse) pops out from behind back	But left behind a mouse!
	Then, Aunt Matilda came back home
Move pinky around	(And what about the cake?)
	That little mouse had helped himself!
Pinky "sniffs" cake	(And how much did he take?)
Nod head affirmatively	The cake was gone! She set a trap!
	(She set a trap, you say?)
Quickly move left hand over right pinky and say "hooray!"	Yes, Aunt Matilda set a trap
	And caught that mouse! (Hooray!)

VARIATION
Children say the responses in parenthesis

Pork Chops and Applesauce

FINGERPLAY
Children are sitting

Pork chops and applesauce!

Rub hands together   Sure sounds good!

"Stir" the pot   Maybe Mom'll fix it—

O I wish she would!

"Butter" left palm with right hand   Serve it with a little bit

Of butter and bread!

Rub stomach   "Yummy in the tummy's" goin'

Make circle in the air near head   'Round my head!

Minnie

FINGERPLAY
Children are sitting

Curl left hand in an open circle. Take out "money" with left hand   Minnie spent her money on a frozen
lemon-lime.

Turn left hand over & shake   Now she hasn't any—not a penny,
not a dime!

"Better save your money, Minnie, maybe
you should try:

Shake finger   There will be another day with other things
to buy!"

Chicken in the Frying Pan

FINGERPLAY
Children are sitting

Left forefinger "in"	Chicken in the frying pan!
Right forefinger "in"	Noodles in the pot!
Rub stomach & lick lips	Sunday dinner's ready
Shake index finger and put in mouth (hot)	And the biscuits are hot!
Make "come on" motion	Everybody hurry, now!
Point to "watch"	Sorry if you're late.
Raise up and sit back down	Sit around the table;
Smile and lick lips	Mother's heaping your plate!

I Rarely Have Soup

FINGERPLAY
Children are sitting

Cup hands together   I rarely have soup when I'm eating at noon:

Slurp, slurp and then watch "drip"   It runs through my fork and spills out of
my spoon!

Move hands back & forth to mouth   I'd rather have something to eat with
my hands,

Rub stomach   Like hotdogs and french fries or pizza
in pans!

Mama's Poppin' Popcorn

FINGERPLAY
Children are sitting

Clap, clap on "popcorn"   Mama's poppin' popcorn!

Clap on "pop"   Hear that popcorn pop!

Rub tummy   How I love to eat it; fill my

*Curl both arms out, overlap hands &
smile*   Bowl up to the top!

Merrie, Merrie

FINGERPLAY
Children are sitting

"Pick" "berries" in front

Merrie, Merrie, pick some berries
And we'll have a lovely pie.

*Shake head firmly "no" and point to
self*

"Me pick berries?" answered Merrie.
"Never! Never! No, not I!"

Shake finger

Berries Merrie will not pick!
Mother, Mother, get the stick!

Sam the Pizza Man

FINGERPLAY
Children are sitting

Hold both hands out, palms up

Sam the Pizza Man put a pizza in the pan,

Dot the air & rub stomach

And he put a lotta sausage on the top.
   (That's good!)
Now, I know if he would only

Put right index finger on chin

Add the cheese and pepperoni,

Shake head "yes"

He would have a nice-a-pizza! Serve it hot!
   (I would!)

Franklin, Franklin

FINGERPLAY
Children are sitting

Shake finger	Franklin, Franklin! Can't you see?!
Curl right hand (cup) & spill over	You have spilled your milk on me!
	Such a reckless kind of kid!
Shake index finger	Are you sorry that you did?
Put finger on chin, wondering	Am I sorry? Well, I guess. . .
Hold both arms out, palms up	I HAVE made an awful mess.
(Said slowly), put hand on chest	I am sor-ri-er, I think,
(Said quickly), shrug	Because I have no milk to drink!

Pollyanna

ACTION VERSE
Children are standing

Pollyanna

Peel "banana"   Ate a banana;

Threw the peeling

Toss "peel" up   On the ceiling

Follow path of "peel" as it falls down with your finger   And before it hit the floor,

Clap and slide one hand out   Pollyanna ran out the door!

Point right and left   Mom and Dad

Hands on hips   (They were mad!)

Motion "come back"   Called her back

Clap on "whack"   And gave her a whack!

Point away   "Go to bed,"

Is what they said.

Shake head "no"   No more banana

For poor Pollyanna!

Said a Fellow

FINGERPLAY
Children are sitting

Cup hand to mouth	Said a fellow, with a shout:
Look right and left	"Is there anyone about?
	I would like a bite to eat—
Rub stomach	Like a bit of bread and meat!"
Cup hand to mouth and say louder	Said a voice a little louder:
	"WE HAVE ONLY FISH HEAD CHOWDER!"
	"Fish head chowder, Mr. Waiter??
Shake head "no"	Never, never!...
Wave bye, bye	...SEE YOU LATER!"

Something Smells Good...Adam

FINGERPLAY
Children are sitting

Sniff, sniff	Something sure smells good!
Sniff again	It's cookies! Mother made 'em!
Hold hands together, begging	"O please, may I
	Have one to try?"
Rub stomach and smile	So sorry! Adam ate 'em!

Home
And Family

What Is the Sound

FINGERPLAY
Children are sitting

Cup hand to ear	What is the sound that I hear in the hall?
Move right finger back & forth	A cuckoo clock ticking away on the wall!
Form hands into circles & look through them	Hiding inside is a wee, little bird,
Cup hand to ear & smile	And a moment ago, it was HE that I heard! "Cuckoo!"

Rickety, Crickety

ACTION VERSE
Children are standing

Rock back & forth on feet	Rickety, crickety, rockety chair,
Sit down slightly	Setting alone at the top of the stair,
Put hand up for "stop" gesture	Waiting for someone to stop for a minute
Rock on feet again	And rickety, crickety, rockety in it!

Esther Passed Her Sister

ACTION VERSE

One child is "Esther". The others stand in a circle with space between each other. "Esther" weaves in and out among the children for the whole rhyme.

Esther passed her sister. Was her sister
running faster?
Was the sister Esther passed the fastest sister
Esther had?
(Yes, the sister passed by Esther was the
fastest one she had!)

My Sister and My Brother

FINGERPLAY
Children are sitting

Clap, clap on each line

My sister and my brother
Are the children of my mother,
And her husband is our father,
And our mother is his wife.

Finger on chin, wondering

How many people are there in our house,
do you suppose?

Finger on nose

If you think you know the answer, put your
finger on your nose!

VARIATION
Count family members on fingers

Charley Needs a Haircut

FINGERPLAY
Children are sitting

"Scissors hair" and shake head "no"	Charley needs a haircut—doesn't wanna go,
Hold up three fingers	Even though the barber has three chairs in a row:
Take down one finger & then another	One for Charley's father, one for Brother Ken,
Move remaining finger back & forth	Another chair for Charley. Will he go or has he been?

Melanie Appleby

FINGERPLAY
Children are sitting

Point away in the distance	Melanie Appleby lives down the street,
Say line in exaggerated way	And everyone always says, "Isn't she sweet?!"
Shake head "no" and point to self	Nobody ever says that about me;
Point to self & then to place from line 1	But, then, I'm a "he," and, of course, she's a "she!"

VARIATION
The name and placement of pronouns can be changed, so the meaning is appropriate for a she or a he.

Molly Milano

FINGERPLAY
Children are sitting

"Play the piano"	Molly Milano, she has a piano.
Repeat	She plays it all day while the family's away.
Hold hands on ears	She plays it at night and the noise is a fright!
Keep hands on ears & rock head back & forth	All the neighbors complain that her pounding's a pain!
	So Molly Milano will sell her piano
Move arms in and out to play drum	And buy a bass drum just to please everyone.
Beat drum harder	Now, what will they say when the drumbeats begin?!
Play piano again	They'll ask her to play her piano again!

Uncle Henry

ACTION VERSE
Children are standing

Hold "steering wheel" Uncle Henry bought a car.
(He bought a car, you say?)
Turn "steering wheel" Yes, Uncle Henry bought a car
A week ago today.

Bend down & turn crank So Uncle Henry cranked the car.
(He cranked the car, you say?)
Bend down & turn crank again Yes, Uncle Henry cranked the car
Turn "steering wheel" left & right And then he drove away.

Turn "steering wheel" sharply to the right Well, Uncle Henry wrecked the car!
(He wrecked the car, you say?)
Repeat motions from line 9 Yes, Uncle Henry wrecked the car
Point to "car" And left it where it lay.

Hold onto "reins" & gallop in a circle Now, Uncle Henry has a horse.
(He has a horse, you say?)
Yes, Uncle Henry has a horse
(UNLESS IT RAN AWAY!).

VARIATION
Children learn & respond with sentences in parenthesis.

98

Were a Chigger

FINGERPLAY
Children are sitting

Show "small" with index finger & thumb	Were a chigger any bigger
Arms out, palms up & shrug	What would everybody do?
Scratch ears & chin	Such an itch a chigger gives you!
Scratch faster	You could scratch yourself in two!

I Rode My Bike

FINGERPLAY
Children are sitting

"Pedal" hands in front	I rode my bike down Downer's Hill
Rub eyes, as if crying	And broke a spoke when I took a spill!

Hey Lady

FINGERPLAY
Children are sitting

Put hands over ears & move head from side to side	"Hey, Lady! Your radio's playing too loud! The neighbors have taken a vote.
Cup hand near mouth	Hear this!
Turn hand	You turn that thing down
Point away	Or get outa town By buggy, by bus, or by boat!
Wave	Bye, Bye!"

Scarecrow

ACTION VERSE
Children are standing

Stand like scarecrows with arms & legs held out stiff

Scarecrow!
Whatta you know?

Look to left and right
Guard the corn and watch it grow!

Open mouth, ah oh!
If the birds fly in to eat,

Wave arms stiffly & stomp feet
I'll wave my arms and stomp my feet!

Ding Dong

FINGERPLAY
Children are sitting

"Ring bell"
DING! DONG!
Tell me, did the school bell ring?

Rest head on hands
Sound asleep,

Shake head "no"
I didn't hear a thing!

Open mouth & put hands on cheeks
O dear me!

Point to "watch"
It's nearly nine o'clock!

Cup hand to mouth
Mother!

Point to foot
Mother, help me find my sock!

A Fox in the Henhouse

One "fox" is inside the large circle. The fox runs around inside the circle the whole time. The "farmer & wife" are outside the circle. They hold hands and walk around the circle. The rest are a circle of chickens holding hands and moving in a circle. At the last line, all stop and stomp their feet.

A fox in the henhouse! O run for your life!

But where is the farmer and where is his wife??

They went to the city to visit their friends.

Now, what do you think will become of the hens??

The fox will devour them; the farmer will moan.

He may love his friends, but he should have stayed home!

Tidy Dyna

Entwine left & right fingers
Roll hands one over the other
Point to another person

Tidy Dyna tied her shoestrings:
Tied the left one to the right!
Took a step and toppled over!
(Did you think that Dyna mite?)

A Woodpecker Pecked

"Peck" left hand with right index finger

Make circle with thumb & index finger

Make circle with other hand & put both up to eyes

A woodpecker pecked on the front of my door.
He pecked from eleven o'clock until four!
The hole that he pecked was so big I could see
His beady, black eyes staring straight in at me!

Jiggle on the Doorknob

Turn hand in small circle
Tap, tap, tap
Cup hands to mouth
(Louder)

Jiggle on the doorknob!
Rattle on the pane!
Holler down the chimney:
"Hey, I think it's gonna rain!"

102

Pollyanna Hid in a Box

ACTION VERSE
Children are standing

Crouch down & cover head with hands	Pollyanna Hid in a box
Quickly open up hands and pop up	And frightened her mother Right out of her sox!
Laugh	She thought it was funny.
Hands on hips	Her mother thought not!
Shake Finger	Watch out, Pollyanna!
Clap hands on "swat"	You may get a swat!

Steven Twice

FINGERPLAY
Children are sitting

Pat head	Steven TWICE stood on his head
Point down	In the middle of his bed!
Shake finger	If he does it anymore,
Roll hands one over the other	He may flip-flop on the floor!

Larry Had a Pillow Fight

FINGERPLAY
Children are sitting

Toss "pillow" in the air	Larry had a pillow fight
Toss "pillow" to right & left	With his sister, Kate, last night.
Put hands on hips	Mom was mad—so was Dad.
Cup hand to mouth & say line louder	"Larry! Kate! Turn out that light!"

Father Bought a Feather Duster

FINGERPLAY
Children are sitting

"Dust"	Father bought a feather duster,
Put right hand down to side	Mother laid it down;
Pat head	Gran'ma sewed it on her hat,
Hold head proudly	And wore it into town!

I Play With My Toys

FINGERPLAY
Children are sitting

Stack "blocks" on lap	I play with my toys and
Put hands up to "shelf"	I put them away.
	My mother expects it;
Shrug	What more can I say?

VARIATION
"Mother" in line 3 can be changed to teacher.

Fun
And Games

A Jack-in-the-Box

ACTION VERSE
Children are standing

Turn around in place

Jump up quickly

A jack-in-the-box is a tricky thing:

Just wind him up if you dare;

And evening or morning without any
warning,

He'll pop up and give you a scare!

VARIATIONS

The teacher says, "I'm closing your lid," and the children stoop. Teacher varies speaking rate from time to time, to let children anticipate the words, "pop up!"

I Can, You Can

FINGERPLAY
Children sit.

They clap on each "can". Repeat the rhyme faster, clapping on each "can" & trying to say it all in one breath.

I can, you can, he can, she can!

Who can? We can! (Yes, they can!)

("Can" what? Say these with one breath!)

VARIATION

First child: I can! (point to self)
Second child: You can! (point to another child)
Third child: He can! (point to boy)
Fourth child: She can! (point to girl)
Class: WHO CAN?
Four solos: We can! (point to themselves)
Class: YES, THEY CAN!

Whittle on a Broomstick

FINGERPLAY
Children are sitting

Whittle left index finger with right hand

Play the "fiddle"

Whittle on a broomstick!

Whittle on a twig!

Fiddle while I whittle!

Will you fiddle a jig?

Is It Thimble

FINGERPLAY
Children are sitting

Hold up right index finger	Is it thimble on a finger,
Hold up left index finger	Or a fimble on a thinger??
Put finger on chin	If I stop and think a minute,
	Then I think that I can say it:
Hold up left index finger & shake head "no"	Not a fimble on a thinger,
Hold up right index finger	But a thimble on a finger!
Smile	Did I say it? Yes, I said it!
Fold arms in front of body	And I think I said it right!

A Merry-Go-Round

Nod head "yes"	A merry-go-round! Shall we take a ride?
Stretch right hand into circle	If you've got a ticket you can!
Jump once into circle	You jump on a horse that goes up and down,
Gallop around the circle	And end up back where you began!

Can a Pig Dance a Jig

ACTION VERSE
Children are standing

Dance jig, in place	Can a pig dance a jig?
Stroke hair	Can a wag wear a wig?
Jog in place	Can a dog do a jog?
Hold "steering wheel"	Can you drive in a fog?
Stand tall	If you can, you're a man;
Shake head "no"	Not a sausage in a pan;
Stroke hair	Not a wag in a wig;
Jog in place	Not a jigging, jogging pig!

My Father and I

ACTION VERSE
Children are standing

My father and I took a wonderful ride

Wow! On a carnival ferris wheel!

Sit down slightly You get in a seat with a place for your feet

Stand up to tippy toes and back to "sitting" And go up and come down with a squeeeeeeeeeeal!

Back up to tippy toes And when you go up and you stop at the top,

Point down You can see all the people below.

Show small with index finger & thumb It's funny, but true: they look smaller than you,

Back down to "sitting" Until, suddenly, back down you go!

Is It True

FINGERPLAY
Children are sitting

Put finger on chin, wondering Is it true, or don't you know?

Flap arms to fly & then shrug shoulders Flies can fly, but crows can't crow!

Bobby Put His Bubble Gum

ACTION VERSE
Children are standing

Move hand from mouth to floor — Bobby put his bubble gum
Underneath the big bass drum.
Struggle with "drum" — When he went to pick it up,
Struggle harder, put it down & wipe brow — The big brass drum was stuck-stuck-stuck!

A Fellow Named Niece

ACTION VERSE
Children are standing

Start with hands on sides. Everyone swing arms front & back — A fellow named Niece
Had a bucket of bolts,
One by one join hands while swinging arms — And he made him a robot
With 99 volts.

While swinging arms, shake head from side to side — The robot was sassy,

One by one drop hands & continue swinging until the end — And so Mr. Niece
Proceeded to take him apart,
Piece by piece!

Whizzin' Frisbee

FINGERPLAY
Children are sitting

Toss "frisbee" in the air Whizzin' frisbee in the air!

Put hand over eyes & look in the distance Now it's gone-I wonder where??

If it landed in a tree

Stretch arms out, palms up Who will get it down for me?

Zoomerang a Boomerang

ACTION VERSE
The children are in a circle.

One child is the maple tree in the center of the circle. This child stands. The outer circle children skip around the circle the whole time. The "maple tree" child shakes a finger at the children as they go by.

Zoomerang a boomerang
Around a maple tree!
Zoomerang a boomerang
But don't hit me!

Somebody Sat on Barnaby's Hat

FINGERPLAY
Children are sitting

Pat head	Somebody sat on Barnaby's hat!
"Climb" hands up both sides of head	It took a bit-of-a-climb:
Fold arms & cross right leg over left	The hat that someone sat upon
Pat head, open mouth	Was on his head at the time!

Dolly Molly

ACTION VERSE
Children are standing

Lay head on hands on the right side	Dolly Molly sleeps all night,
Lay head on hands on the left side	And then she sleeps all day.
Hands on hips	"O golly, Dolly Molly, dear,
Shake finger	Don't sleep your life away!"
Left hand is "bread", right hand spreads butter	"I'll make some butter sandwiches
Hold up two fingers	And lemonade for two,
Clap hands, Yay!	And we can have a picnic. I
Point to another person	Would like that! Wouldn't you?"

Listen! Listen!

FINGERPLAY
Children are sitting

Close eyes	Listen! Listen! Close your eyes!
Open eyes & mouth, in surprise	Open up! Surprise! Surprise!
	Mother brought it from the store.
Turn hand to open door	Help her get it through the door,
Hold on with right hand, then left	Two on one side—two, the other,
Move left left hand, then right	Sister, sister—brother, brother.
Strain	Is it heavy? O gee whiz!
Wipe brow	Is it heavy?! Yes, it is!
	Such a box I've never seen!
Put finger on chin	What can such a big box mean?
	If you guess what's hid inside,
Point to someone	You can be the first to ride!

Over and Under

ACTION VERSE
The children stand in a circle.

One child is in the center and performs the motions of the rhyme using the children in the circle.

Over and under,
In front of, beside;
Inside and outside
Are places to hide.

On and behind
And among and between
Are places to be
Where I cannot be seen!

FINGERPLAY
The right hand performs the motions of the rhyme, using the left hand and fingers as a prop.

VARIATION
Real objects can be used to make this a more concrete learning experience.

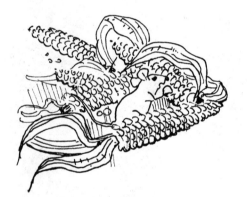

If a Baby Blew a Bubble

FINGERPLAY
Children are sitting

Blow up cheeks	If a baby blew a bubble,
Put finger on chin	What would happen, would you say?
Clap on "burst"	Would the baby bubble burst
Blow	Or would the bubble blow away??

Color
And Numbers

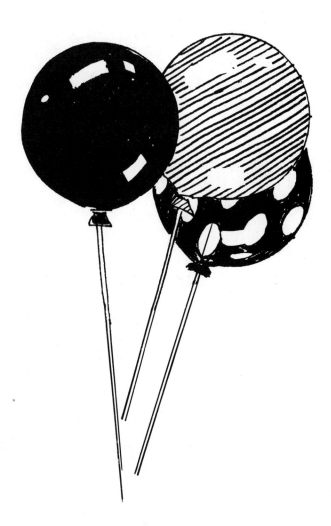

Step One, Step Two

ACTION VERSE
Children are standing

Step on one & two	Step one! Step two!
	I'm up with you!
Step on three and four	Step three and four!
Make "come on" motion	Let's walk some more!
Step 5,6,7 & 8	Step five and six and seven and eight;
"open gate"	And, now, we're going through the gate!
Hold up two fingers	Just two steps more,
	We're at the door!
Step on 9 & 10	Step nine and ten:
Step, step in place	We're home again!

FINGERPLAY

Start rhyme on the left hand, held up with palm facing in. Use right index finger to point to each finger. Move from finger to finger on each number in the rhyme. Start with the left thumb and move over to the right hand, so that the rhyme ends with the right thumb.

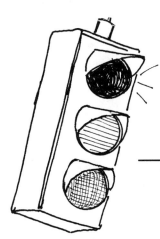

Standing on the Sidewalk

ACTION VERSE

Children are standing in 2 lines facing each other

	Standing on the sidewalk
Tap toes with arms folded	(Need to cross the street),
Tap toes	Waiting for the green before
	I move my feet. Oh,
Point	I can see the red light!
Hold hand in "stop" position	(Red means "Stop!")
Walk, skip, or hop to opposite line's position	When I see the green light, I
	Can walk, skip, hop!

On Lavender Avenue

ACTION VERSE

The children move in a circle with tiny steps and holding their hands near their mouths. At the last line, everyone stops and says, "squeak, squeak!"

On Lavender Avenue Leander lives
With a cat in a lavender house.
The cat isn't real, or he'd have a good meal
'Cause Leander, you see, IS A MOUSE!

Oliver Brown

FINGERPLAY
Children are sitting

Point away   Oliver Brown was sent to bed
Open mouth & cover with hand   After he painted his brother red!
Hold chin in hand, wondering   Maybe blue would be all right;
Put hands on cheeks   But red? Not red! O what a sight!

Barney Has a Basketball

ACTION VERSE
Children are standing

Hold "ball"	Barney has a basketball.
Point to colors on "ball"	It's red and white and blue;
Dribble "ball"	And, if you play the game with him,
Pass "ball" into the middle	He'll pass the ball to you.
Catch "ball"	You catch it and you dribble,
Shoot basket	And you run and put it in.
Hold up two fingers	"That's 'two' for us and 'none' for them:
Yay! Jump up	I think we're gonna win!"

My Favorite Color Is Pink

FINGERPLAY
Children are sitting

Finger on chin, confused	My favorite color is pink, I think;
Smile	But red is pretty, too.
Extend right hand out, then left	It's one or the other unless I discover
Shrug shoulders	I'm suddenly partial to blue!

Pollyanna! See What She's Got

FINGERPLAY
Children are sitting

Point	Pollyanna! See what she's got?!
Dot air	A purple bandana with pink polka dots!
Rest head on hands	She wears it to school and she wears it to bed.
Put on "bandana"	She wears a bandana to cover her head.
Shrug shoulders	You may think it's funny (or, maybe, don't care)
"Scissor" hair with 2 fingers	But poor Pollyanna has cut off her hair!

Bobby Had a Big Balloon

FINGERPLAY
Children are sitting

Blow up cheeks

Bobby had a big balloon
Much bigger than his head!

Hold hands out on both sides of mouth
Move hands out slowly

It wasn't green; it wasn't blue;
His big balloon was red!

Hold hands up high with closed fist

He tied it with a piece of string
And held it way up high;

Open hand and look up

But, when he opened up his hand,
It floated to the sky!

Put hand over eyes
Point far away
Point finger on chin
Shake head "yes"

He watched it slowly disappear
Completely out of sight.
Will someone find that big balloon??
I kinda think they might!

A Few is Not So Many

FINGERPLAY
Children are sitting

Hold hands slightly apart ("a few")	A few is not so many
Move hands out a bit & then back	And more is more than some;
Move hands way out	But if you've got the most, you've got
Chew, chew, chew	A lotta bubble gum!

How Many People

FINGERPLAY
Children are sitting

Hold up left arm (steeple)	How many people
Climb "steeple" with 2 fingers	Could climb up a steeple,
Stop at heel of hand	Could climb to the very tip-top?
	Could you??
Shake head "no"	"Oh not many people
Climb down quickly	Could climb up a steeple,
Point to self & shake head "no"	And I'm one of those who could not!
	So what?"

ACTION VERSE
The children stand in a circle, crouched down. Stretch up slowly and then stretch arms up (first stanza).
Shake head "no", crouch back down and clap, clap (second stanza).

Old Lady Brady

FINGERPLAY
Children are sitting

Stroke "whiskers" on face	Old Lady Brady has twenty-four cats
Say meow	And they were meowing last night. (Meow!)
Hold out hands together, palms up	She gave them a fish—a fish on a dish
Hold up 1 finger & bite	And every last one had a bite! (One bite!)

Wickware

ACTION VERSE
Children are standing

Take twelve steps (in place)	Wickware Climbed the stair;
Turn around and take 12 steps	Turned around And went back down.
Turn around again	Counted till there were no more,
Clap 24 times	And what there were were twenty-four.

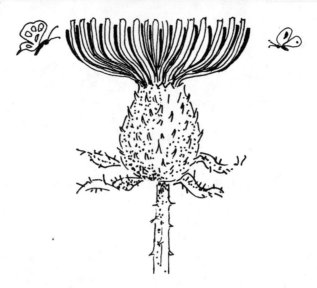

Myrtle Picked a Purple Thistle

ACTION VERSE
Children are standing

Bend over and pick up "thistle"   Myrtle picked a purple thistle.

Curl left arm out & around & place   Heidi hid it in a sack.
"thistle" in this place

Put fingers in mouth to whistle   If you see that thistle, whistle!

Hold both arms out and in front of   Myrtle wants her thistle back!
body

124

Index